WHEN
TIME BEGAN

WHEN TIME BEGAN

The Creation for Beginning Readers

Genesis 1:1—2:3 FOR CHILDREN

by Mary Blount Christian
illustrated by Aline Cunningham

I CAN READ A BIBLE STORY
Series Editor: Dorothy Van Woerkom

Publishing House
St. Louis

IN MEMORY OF
BELLE AND JIM DILL

Concordia Publishing House, St. Louis, Missouri
Copyright © 1976 Concordia Publishing House

Manufactured in the United States of America

Library of Congress Cataloging in Publication Data

Christian, Mary Blount.
    When time began.

    (I can read a Bible story)
    SUMMARY: Easy-to-read account of the creation.
    1. Creation—Juvenile literature. [1. Creation. 2. Bible stories—O. T.]
I. Cunningham, Aline. II. Title.
BS651.C47   222′.11′09505   76-14359
ISBN 0-570-07308-1
ISBN 0-570-07302-2 pbk.

Before time began

there was only darkness.

Everywhere, black waters

whirled and swirled.

They were blown by a great wind

that never stopped and

never slowed.

There were no ears to hear,

but God's.

There were no eyes to see,

but God's.

There was nothing

and no one

but God, and the black waters,

and the darkness.

"Let the world have light,"

God said.

And a soft glow appeared

all around.

God said, "It is good."

He called the light *day*.

He called the darkness *night*.

He parted them from each other.

After the evening, it was night.
And this was the end
of the first day
of the world.

Morning of
the second day came.
Again God saw the dark waters
blown by the wind.
He made a great arch
to part the waters.

There was dark whirling water
above.

There was dark swirling water
below.

But the arch was bright
and peaceful.

God called the arch *heaven*.

Evening and night came.

And again it was morning.

This was the third day.

God parted the waters that were

under the arch of heaven.

Mountains and valleys

appeared

where the waters had been.

"I will call the dry land *earth*,"
God said.
"And I will call the waters *seas*.
But the earth
is too bare," God said.
He told plants and trees
to grow.

Then green grass grew
in the brown earth.
The grass dipped and nodded
in the wind.

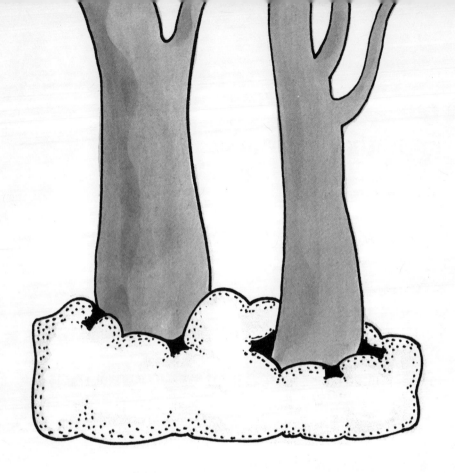

Trees pushed

their tall trunks

through

the soft earth.

From the tall trunks,

branches grew.

They were filled with

green leaves and

fruits of red and yellow and orange.

Each carried seeds of its own kind.

Flowers of many colors

grew all around.

They moved with the wind,

and the air was full

of their sweet smells.

Night came, then morning.

It was the fourth day.

God made two great lights.

He called the biggest light *sun*.

"You shall rule the day," God said.

The sun grew stronger and stronger,

until its warm glow

made the fruit ripen.

The flowers

and trees

reached toward the sun.

They grew even

stronger and sweeter.

God called the smaller light *moon*.

"You shall rule the night," God said.

The moon's silver light

fell over the quiet earth.

God made many other lights.

He put them in the night sky.

God called them *stars*.

"The stars shall be signs

of the seasons," God said.

There was night,

then morning again.

And it was the fifth day.

God looked at the waters around

the green earth.

"Let the waters be filled
with many living creatures,"
God said.
The great whale
and the tiny minnow
swam side by side.

The shrimp and the sea horse
darted by,
making ripples in the water.

The starfish and the crab
crawled slowly
over the sandy bottom of the sea.

God looked at the air above earth.

It was empty.

"Let the air be filled with birds,"
God said.

And the air was filled
with eagle and dove,
with redbird and sparrow.
Their wings fluttered
against the wind.
Their songs floated over the earth.
God smiled.
He said, "This is good."
He told them all to have
families—
each of its own kind.

The morning came,

and it was the sixth day.

Fishes swam in the water.

Birds flew in the sky.

But on the land,

there was nothing.

God sent animals

and things that crawled

to live on the earth.

Deer played among the trees.

Their feet

made almost no sound

on the soft ground.

Cows and sheep and goats
ate the green grass.

Snakes and lizards

crawled

onto rocks

in the sun.

The lion lifted its head and roared.

The elephant lifted its trunk

to answer.

God saw. He was pleased.

He told them all to have

families—

each of its own kind.

From the dust,

God made man and woman.

He made them to look like Himself.

God blew His own breath

into their lungs.

Man and woman came to life.
They looked around them
at the world God had made.
They felt the warm sun
on their bodies.

They heard the songs of the birds.

And they felt the grass

under their feet.

Their voices

rang out in happy laughter.

And God was pleased.

"You shall rule
over the fish in the sea,"
God told them.
"You shall rule over the birds
in the air.
And you shall rule over the
animals on the land," God said.

Night came, then morning.

And it was the seventh day.

God blessed that day.

He called it holy.

He told man and woman

to work six days,

and to rest on the seventh day.

God looked at all He had made.

He was pleased.

"I have worked six days," God said.

"On the seventh day I shall rest."

On the seventh day

man and woman

would give thanks to God.

And so it was,

in the beginning.

ABOUT THE AUTHOR

Mary Blount Christian graduated from the University of Houston with a degree in journalism and was a reporter and columnist before becoming a free-lance writer. She has written eleven books for young children, including *The Goosehill Gang* series for Concordia, *Devin and Goliath, No Dogs Allowed, Jonathan,* and *The First Sign of Winter.* Her book for middle readers, *Sebastian, Super Sleuth,* is the first in a series about a dog detective. Ms. Christian is a book critic for the HOUSTON POST and is producing a series of programs on children's literature called "Children's Bookshelf" for Public Television. She lives in Houston with her writer-husband and their three children.